He Is Witn Us Always

BROTHER FRANÇOIS FONTANIÉ, CFR

Our Sunday Visitor
Huntington, Indiana

Nihil Obstat
Msgr. Michael Heintz, Ph.D.
Censor Librorum

Imprimatur
✠ Kevin C. Rhoades
Bishop of Fort Wayne-South Bend
October 31, 2019

The *Nihil Obstat* and *Imprimatur* are official declarations that a book is free from doctrinal or moral error. It is not implied that those who have granted the Nihil Obstat and Imprimatur agree with the contents, opinions, or statements expressed.

Our Sunday Visitor Publishing Division
Our Sunday Visitor, Inc.
200 Noll Plaza
Huntington, IN 46750
1-800-348-2440

ISBN: 978-1-68192-487-8 (Inventory No. T2377)
1. RELIGION—Christianity—Catholic. 2. JUVENILE NONFICTION—Religion—Devotional & Prayer.
3. JUVENILE NONFICTION—Religion—Christianity—Christian Life.

LCCN: 2019953674

Cover and interior design: Chelsea Alt
Cover and interior art: Brother François Fontanié, CFR

PRINTED IN THE UNITED STATES OF AMERICA

FOR MAŸLIS, MY GODDAUGHTER

"Come with me! We will visit the Blessed Sacrament."

"The Blessed Sacrament is the Eucharist."

"Brother François, please tell us about the Eucharist."
"All right!"

The Eucharist is

A DEEP TRUTH,

so deep that we cannot understand it completely.

Look at this hole in the sand.

You will never finish filling it up with water!
In the same way, we will never finish
understanding the Eucharist.

The Eucharist is

AN ENDLESS
GIFT OF LOVE.

You see, God created the earth, the ocean,
the trees, and the animals, all for us.
But he wanted to give us even more.

God became a baby for us.
But he wanted to give us even more.

Jesus died on the cross for us.
But he wanted to give us even more.

He wanted to give us
more than enough.

That is why Jesus made himself food for us.
This food is the Eucharist.

The Eucharist is
JESUS.

After his resurrection, before he went into heaven,
Jesus promised his friends:
"Know that I am with you always."

Jesus kept his promise.

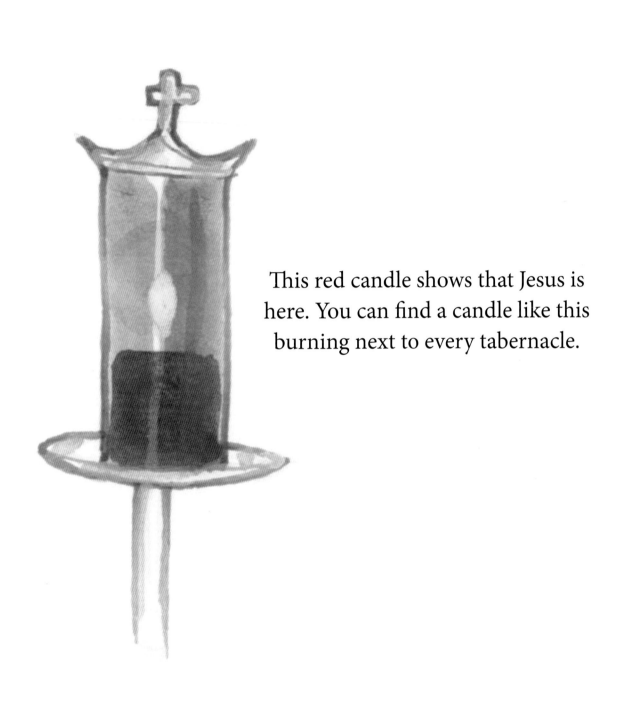

This red candle shows that Jesus is here. You can find a candle like this burning next to every tabernacle.

In the Eucharist,

JESUS CHOOSES TO BE POOR.

Look at this poor man.
Jesus chooses to live in this poor man.

Like the poor man, this bread is poor.

Now look how Jesus chooses to be poor.
Do you see the bread in the hands of the priest?

During Mass, the priest celebrates Jesus' death and resurrection.

At that moment,
this poor piece of bread
and this cup of wine
become the Body and
Blood of Jesus.

The Eucharist is

A WAY TO SAY "THANK YOU"

to God.

At Mass, we can think about our week.
We say "thank you" to Jesus for everything.

Each time we say
"thank you," we bring a
gift to Jesus.

Jesus loves when we offer him everything,
even our sins, mistakes, and worries.
He changes all of it into good.

In the Eucharist, we all become

ONE.

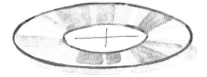

When we receive communion, Jesus is inside us.

We are one with Jesus.

We also are one with every other person who receives Jesus.

All together, we become the Body of Christ more and more.

So let us

SPEND TIME

with the Blessed Sacrament.

Look at these sunflowers.

Because they are always turning toward the sun,
they end up *looking like* the sun.

We are like those sunflowers, and Jesus is like the sun. When we turn toward him in the Eucharist, he looks upon us with love and makes us beautiful, just as he is beautiful.

Dear parents,

This book is for you as well.

I hope you find it to be a valuable resource for teaching and sharing the gift of the Eucharist with your children.

The Eucharist is the source and summit of our Faith. It is thus essential to your child's spiritual growth to learn at a young age to approach Our Lord, present in this Sacrament, with trust and love.

We are all children before the mystery of the Eucharist. Let us dive deeply into this relationship of love.

God bless you and your family.

Br. François, CFR